INDIAN BLOOD

A R Gurney

BROADWAY PLAY PUBLISHING INC
New York
www.broadwayplaypublishing.com
info@broadwayplaypublishing.com

INDIAN BLOOD

Cover photo by James Leynse
First printing: November 2006
I S B N: 978-0-88145-321-8
Book design: Marie Donovan
Word processing: Microsoft Word
Typographic controls: Ventura Publisher
Typeface: Palatino
Printed and bound in the U S A

INDIAN BLOOD opened in New York City 9 August 2006 at the 59E59 Theater. The play was produced by Primary Stages (Casey Childs, Executive Producer; Andrew Leynse, Artistic Director; and Elliot Fox, Managing Director). The cast and creative contributors were:

EDDIE	Charles Socarides
MR KENYON	Matthew Arkin
LAMBERT	Jeremy Blackman
MRS GARVER	Katharine McGrath
JANE	Rebecca Luker
HARVEY	Jack Gilpin
ANNIE	Katharine McGrath
GRANDMOTHER	Pamela Payton-Wright
GRANDFATHER	John McMartin
MRS STAWICKI	Katharine McGrath
UNCLE PAUL	Matthew Arkin

Director	Mark Lamos
Set design	John Arnone
Costume design	Ann Hould-Ward
Lighting design	Howell Brinkley
Original music	John Gromada
Sound design	John Gromada
Projection design	Leah Gelpe
Production stage manager	Frederic H Orner

SET

There may possibly be other ways to present this play, but the original New York production concentrated on making it as simple and fluid as possible. The show curtain displayed a projection of a simplified map of New York State, highlighting Buffalo, the Erie Canal to Albany, and the Hudson River flowing on down to New York City. As the houselights dimmed, quiet music piano chords played under a series of tinted postcard views of Buffalo displayed the city in its prime. The drop rose to reveal a neutral but formal space, against the back wall of which projections of various window frames would define the different interiors during the course of the play. A number of bentwood chairs, moved by the actors into various arrangements, provided the only furniture, except for the Grandfather's leather swivel chair and the grandmother's antique wingback. Sound and lighting effects amplified the scenes. The only prop throughout was a blank piece of paper which served as Eddie's drawing. All other stage business was mimed, but as simply as possible. The costumes, on the other hand, explicitly evoked the mid-1940s, from the hats on down to the galoshes.

The play is dedicated to Mark Lamos
and everyone else involved in the original production.

(The drop lifts to reveal the actors sitting and eating, as if around a formal dining room table. EDDIE *gets up and turns to the audience as the other actors freeze. He should be about sixteen.)*

EDDIE: *(To audience)* This is a play about me when I was growing up in the city of Buffalo, New York, which began as an Indian trading post at the mouth of Lake Erie. Because of the Erie Canal, we became the Gateway to the Midwest and the Queen City of the Great Lakes, but nowadays, the city is in trouble so my History teacher calls us the Mistake on the Lake.

(The actors behind him resume eating and silently conversing.)

EDDIE: O K, but in 1946, which is when I'm talking about, we are still a big, bustling city with a lot going on. For example, we have plays here on their way to or from New York, with major stars, and large casts, and plenty of scenery, and they stay here for two or three weeks at the Erlanger Theater.

My parents are subscribers, and on opening nights, they wear evening clothes, and sit in the fourth row, and have a drink with their friends during intermission, and sometimes go dancing afterwards at the Statler Hotel across the street from the theatre. My History teacher says that now the war's over, people will live differently, and go to plays differently, and plays will be different then, too....

(Sound of a school bell, then of the scraping of chairs and the chatter of boys leaving at the end of a class. The actors take

chairs and leave, except for MR KENYON, *a schoolmaster, who calls to* EDDIE *who is leaving, too.)*

MR KENYON: *(As he erases the blackboard)* Eddie!

EDDIE: *(Stopping)* Me?

MR KENYON: You answer to the name of Eddie, don't you?

EDDIE: Yes sir.

MR KENYON: I'd like you to stay after class for a moment, please.

EDDIE: I'll be late for History.

MR KENYON: History can wait, Eddie.

*(*EDDIE *waits;* MR KENYON *continues to write on the board, as if preparing for the next class.)*

MR KENYON: Lambert tells me that he had difficulty translating his Latin today.

EDDIE: Oh really?

MR KENYON: He says you were distracting him.

EDDIE: What? That squealer!

MR KENYON: Hold on now.

EDDIE: I was way in the back row!

MR KENYON: He says you were making the other boys laugh.

EDDIE: That stool pigeon!

MR KENYON: No name-calling, please.

EDDIE: It's not my fault if people laugh.

MR KENYON: It becomes your fault if you *make* them laugh.

EDDIE: Lambert was taking forever with that Latin. He couldn't even find the verb.

MR KENYON: Lambert found the verb immediately, Eddie. What Lambert was trying to do was cope with an unfamiliar construction called the ablative absolute *(Indicating it on the blackboard)* ...which you may come across yourself when you get around to doing your homework.

EDDIE: Why do we have to study Latin anyway?

MR KENYON: Take that up with your parents.

EDDIE: Learning all those declensions and stuff. Why do we have to learn things that don't mean anything?

MR KENYON: Latin meant something to millions of people for hundreds of years, Eddie. And apparently it still means something to Lambert.

EDDIE: Lambert's just gunning for a good grade.

MR KENYON: He's your cousin, isn't he?

EDDIE: Second cousin only.

MR KENYON: Which means?

EDDIE: Our grandmothers are sisters.

MR KENYON: Mister Kaiser tells me you had a serious scuffle with him two days ago during recess. Why don't you two get along?

EDDIE: You want to know?

MR KENYON: I'd like very much to know, Eddie.

EDDIE: It's our Indian blood.

MR KENYON: Your Indian blood?

EDDIE: We've got Indian blood in us, sir. I'm part Seneca, Lambert's a Tuscarora. The Senecas hate the Tuscaroras since time immemorial..

MR KENYON: Oh for God's sake, Eddie.

EDDIE: No, it's true! It explains a lot of my disruptive behavior. Deep inside, I harbor a profound grudge against the customs of the white man. Unlike Lambert, who's trying to adopt.

MR KENYON: He's trying to *adapt*, Eddie....

EDDIE: Whatever he's trying, it makes me go on the warpath.

MR KENYON: Let's get down to brass tacks, Eddie. Lambert says he saw you drawing a picture while he was translating his Latin.

EDDIE: What picture, sir?

MR KENYON: A picture you showed the other boys.

EDDIE: Oh well, that was just—

MR KENYON: I wonder if you'd show it to me, Eddie.

EDDIE: I don't know where it is, sir.

MR KENYON: Lambert said you put it in your pocket when the bell rang.

EDDIE: That stoolie! That fink!

MR KENYON: Give me the picture, Eddie, or you and I will be making an immediate visit to the office of the Headmaster. *(Pause)* I'm waiting.

*(*EDDIE *reluctantly reaches unto his pocket, produces a folded piece of paper.)*

MR KENYON: *(Taking it)* Thank you very much. *(He unfolds it carefully, registers restrained shock.)* Perhaps you'd like to explain this drawing to me, Eddie.

EDDIE: Explain it?

MR KENYON: Yes. I see here two naked figures. Who are they supposed to be?

EDDIE: O K. The man is Injun Joe, from *Tom Sawyer*, by Mark Twain, which we read in seventh grade.

MR KENYON: I see. Because you have him wearing an Indian headdress.

EDDIE: Right.

MR KENYON: Even though you have him wearing nothing else.

EDDIE: O K. Yes.

MR KENYON: And who is the lovely lady?

EDDIE: That's Glinda the Good from *The Wizard of Oz*. The book, not the movie where they turn her into a fussy old lady.

MR KENYON: How am I supposed to know who she is, Eddie, when she is also not wearing any clothes.

EDDIE: You can tell by her magic wand.

MR KENYON: Ah, I see. And are we to assume that these two figures are about to make love?

EDDIE: I guess.

MR KENYON: You guess, Eddie? Wouldn't you say that Injun Joe looks immediately prepared to make love to Glinda the Good?

EDDIE: O K. Yes.

MR KENYON: Yes. And are these words in these little clouds above their heads supposed to be what they're saying?

EDDIE: You know that anyway.

MR KENYON: Never mind what I know, Eddie. *(Hands the paper back to* EDDIE*)* Read me, please, what they are saying.

EDDIE: Out loud, sir?

MR KENYON: Out loud. So we can hear how they sound as public utterances.

*(*EDDIE *mumbles)*

MR KENYON: I can't quite hear what Injun Joe is saying, Eddie.

EDDIE: *(Grimly)* He says, "I want to have sexual intercourse with you, baby doll."

MR KENYON: Yes. And Glinda the Good replies?

EDDIE: Sir...

MR KENYON: Go on, Eddie.

EDDIE: She's saying, "Eeek!"

MR KENYON: Yes. "Eeek". And what else?

EDDIE: *(Defiantly)* She's saying, "Your big dong would never fit into my tiny twat."

(Pause)

MR KENYON: Give me that drawing, Eddie. *(Taking it again)* I understand your father serves on the board of trustees of this school. And the Buffalo Evening News tells me that your mother is again running the annual drive to support our fine philharmonic orchestra.

EDDIE: Yes sir.

MR KENYON: *(Sitting in a chair, as if at desk)* How do you suppose your parents will respond to a drawing like this?

EDDIE: I hope they never see it, sir.

MR KENYON: As indeed they won't. *(He tears the drawing into small pieces.) Sic semper* pornography! *(Puts the pieces in his jacket pocket)*

EDDIE: Whew... Thank you, sir. Very much.

MR KENYON: Whatever possessed you to draw something like that.

EDDIE: My Indian blood, sir.

MR KENYON: Ah. Of course. Which is why you made your hero Injun Joe.

EDDIE: That's it.

MR KENYON: Yes well, perhaps you can call on your Indian blood when you run the gauntlet, Eddie. Isn't that what Indians do when they're captured? Don't they have to run the gauntlet?

EDDIE: Sometimes. If they're captured by a hostile tribe.

MR KENYON: Well now you have a gauntlet to run, too, Eddie. Because it is my duty to tell the headmaster how you disturbed this class. And it will be his duty to suspend you from school for an appropriate period.

EDDIE: That means my family *will* find out!

MR KENYON: Exactly. That's the gauntlet you'll have to run, Eddie. *(Gets up)* So perhaps, as you run it, you will learn two important lessons: one, not to draw lewd pictures which distract hard-working students from their intellectual obligations. And two, not to blame your own depraved imagination on our red-skinned brothers. Now go catch up with History. *(He goes.)*

EDDIE: *(Calling after him)* But sir! *(Turning to audience, taking off his school jacket)* You can see why I didn't want to be home when the headmaster called, so after school I rode my bike over to Ted Garver's house just to hack around and generally avoid the issue...

(Sound of a ping pong game in progress offstage; a record player playing a somewhat scratched version of Big Crosby's I'll Be Home for Christmas.*)*

EDDIE: And guess who was down in the Garver's rumpus room, hanging around the ping-pong table, hoping someone would ask him to play? *(Calling off)* Hey Lambert!

*(*LAMBERT *backs on, as if watching a ping-pong game.)*

LAMBERT: You said something, Eddie?

EDDIE: I said something to you, Lambert, you stupid shit. Squealing to Kenyon , you shitty bastard.

LAMBERT: I couldn't concentrate on the Latin.

EDDIE: You couldn't concentrate on your own pecker, Lambert. You got me into real trouble, whether you know it or not.

LAMBERT: I wanted to do my Latin.

EDDIE: Let me tell you something about the Tuscarora Indians, Lambert.

LAMBERT: *(Walking away)* I 'm not interested, Eddie.

EDDIE: *(Shoving him)* They were sneaky bastards from the word go. It was a Tuscarora who betrayed a Seneca scouting party during the French and Indian War.

LAMBERT: Oh go blow, Eddie!

EDDIE: *(Grabbing him)* Hold it, pal!

(They start wrestling.)

LAMBERT: Get off me!

*(*EDDIE *gets on top, grabs a tuft of* LAMBERT*'s hair.)*

EDDIE: *(To audience)* My Indian blood is really boiling! I feel like scalping the guy! Seriously! I could do it!

*(*MRS GARVER *hurries in.)*

MRS GARVER: Boys! Boys! Stop it this instant! This is a rumpus room, not the island of Iwo Jima.

(The boys get to their feet, brush themselves off.)

EDDIE: Hi, Mrs Garver.

LAMBERT: *(Brushing himself off)* Sorry, Mrs Garver.

MRS GARVER: Eddie: your mother telephoned. She wants you home immediately.

EDDIE: *(To her; innocently)* Oh really? I wonder why.

MRS GARVER: Lambert, you come with me. You need a touch of witch hazel on that mouth of yours. Otherwise you'll end up with a very fat lip.

EDDIE: Which means you'll look even more like the creep you really are, Lambert.

(They start to fight again.)

MRS GARVER: Now, now, Eddie...

*(*LAMBERT *cuffs him.)*

MRS GARVER: Come, Lambert.

LAMBERT: I'll get you for this, Eddie!

EDDIE: *(Calling after him)* Crawl back to your reservation, Lambert!

MRS GARVER: Anger turneth away the heart, boys.

EDDIE: *(To audience)* Mrs Garver teaches Sunday School down at Trinity Church.

MRS GARVER: *(As she and* LAMBERT *go)* Go home now, Eddie.

EDDIE: I will, Mrs Garver. I definitely plan to. *(To audience)* But before I did, Ted Garver and some of the other guys asked me about my drawing, because some of them hadn't seen it, because they were taking Spanish instead of Latin, the lucky ducks. So rather than describe it, I drew the whole thing again. And like a real jerk, I even put my signature on it, the way artists do. But when I looked at what I'd done, the drawing didn't look that good, frankly. Good drawing takes time, and I was in a hurry. The hands looked lousy, for example. You can't draw hands in a hurry. Anyway, I left the drawing there because Ted swore he'd burn it in the incinerator so Mrs Garver couldn't see it. Then I went home.

(JANE, EDDIE*'s mother, comes on, wiping her hands on her apron.)*

JANE: ...And the headmaster said you can't go back to school until after Christmas vacation.

EDDIE: That's over three weeks!

JANE: Exactly, Eddie. And you have to default from the chess tournament, and forego hockey practice until January, and you can't go anywhere near the school, not even for the varsity games on Friday nights.

EDDIE: Oh Jeez!

JANE: Furthermore, I have to drive over to the school every morning and pick up your homework assignments, and turn them in the next day, which somewhat cramps my style, frankly, because I do my grocery telephoning in the morning, as well as my fund-raising calls for the orchestra.

EDDIE: Sorry, Mom.

JANE: Yes well, that must have been quite a picture you drew.

EDDIE: It wasn't so bad.

JANE: Would you describe it for me?

EDDIE: No.

JANE: At least tell me what made you draw it.

EDDIE: My Indian blood.

JANE: Oh phooey.

EDDIE: I can't help my heritage.

JANE: I'm tired of hearing that, Eddie. You sound like a broken record.

EDDIE: Well it's true.

JANE: All I can say is don't pull that excuse on your father.

EDDIE: I'm not that dumb.

JANE: Sometimes I wonder

EDDIE: *(To audience)* And then my father came home....

*(*HARVEY *comes on. He hands his overcoat to* JANE *as he kisses her.)*

HARVEY: Well, Eddie, I hear you've been dabbling in the visual arts.

JANE: Word travels fast.

HARVEY: They were talking about it down at the club.

JANE: Already?

HARVEY: Young Jack Prentice, who's in Eddie's Latin class, was talking about it in the locker room after his Tuesday squash game with his father.

EDDIE: Jack didn't even see the picture. He was sitting way across the room.

HARVEY: Well he certainly heard about it. And thought it was riotously funny. Which I do not. I'm extremely disappointed in you, Eddie.

EDDIE: What else is new?

HARVEY: What did you say, young man.

EDDIE: Nothing.

HARVEY: Yes well it sounds thoroughly repulsive.

EDDIE: May we change the subject, please?

HARVEY: It's rather difficult to change the subject when confronting totally uncivilized behavior.

JANE: Oh Harvey, it's not the end of the world.

HARVEY: I'm not thinking of myself. I'm thinking of my mother.

JANE: I should have known.

HARVEY: Eddie, did you ever, for one minute, consider what this might do to your grandmother?

JANE: Oh Harvey, for Heaven's sake! It's water over the dam.

HARVEY: The boy's been expelled from school!

JANE: Not expelled. Suspended.

HARVEY: Even that would break my mother's heart.

JANE: Oh now really.

HARVEY: It would literally break her heart. Your grandmother has a very bad heart, Eddie.

JANE: I'm not sure I believe that.

HARVEY: And are you a medical expert, darling? Is there a framed medical degree hanging over your dressing room table?

JANE: Doctor Russell says she's as strong as an ox.

HARVEY: I doubt very much if Doctor Russell likened my dear mother unto an ox. If it turns out he did, I can guarantee he won't be her doctor much longer.

JANE: Your mother need never know about this, Harvey. She lives in a world of her own.

HARVEY: She could find out. We live in a small town.

EDDIE: We're the thirteenth largest city in the United States, Pop!

JANE: Exactly! And we have one of the finest symphony orchestras in the entire country.

HARVEY: Yes, but within our particular group, we have managed to preserve many of the virtues of a small community.

JANE: We're both big and small. How about that?

HARVEY: Whatever we are, I don't want my dear mother to be confronted with any more adversity. She has lived through two World Wars and four elections of Franklin D Roosevelt.

JANE: My heart bleeds, Harvey.

HARVEY: Yes well she deserves some peace in her remaining years. So: if she should hear that you're not in school, Eddie, the reason will be... *(He thinks.)* ...the reason will be...you're doing independent study. Have you got that, Eddie?

EDDIE: You want me to lie?

HARVEY: I do not. You're going to be studying here at home by yourself, aren't you?

EDDIE: Yes.

HARVEY: Then you're doing independent study. It's as simple as that.

*(*EDDIE *glances to* JANE *for help.)*

JANE: *(Helplessly)* I'd better do something about dinner. *(She goes.)*

EDDIE: I'd better start my independent homework. *(Starts off)*

HARVEY: Eddie ...

*(*EDDIE *stops.)*

HARVEY: Are you becoming a wise guy, Eddie?

EDDIE: Because I'm doing my homework?

HARVEY: I'm speaking more generally, Eddie. I have the sense that you're fast becoming a wise guy. *(He makes himself a drink.)* Am I right to make that assumption?

EDDIE: I don't know.

HARVEY: I do know. And so do some others. People are beginning to notice that you're becoming just a little bit fresh.

EDDIE: What people?

HARVEY: Well, Mrs Mathewson, for one. She happened to be one of the hostesses at dancing school last week and she saw you purposely get out of step during the grand march. Which caused others behind you to do the same.

EDDIE: That means I've got leadership qualities, Pop.

HARVEY: That's exactly the kind of smart-aleck remark I'm talking about. When someone gets too big for his britches around here, Eddie, the word spreads very rapidly. Charley the barber who cuts our hair hears about it. Miss Bacon who cleans our teeth hears about it. Slip Kreger who runs the exercise room down at the club hears about it, and you can be sure that they all register quiet dismay. No one is fond of a wise guy, Eddie.

EDDIE: O K. O K.

HARVEY: What's more, you are now a fourth former at the Nichols School. In two more years, you will be applying to college, which I sincerely hope will be Yale University. But I'm not at all sure that Yale accepts wise guys.

EDDIE: I said O K, Pop.

(The sound of telephone ringing offstage.)

HARVEY: *(Calling off)* If that's for Eddie, Jane, say that he is having a crucial discussion with his father! *(To* EDDIE*)* Have you thought about military school, Eddie?

EDDIE: *Military* school?

HARVEY: I've been making inquiries, Eddie, and apparently there is an excellent military school named Valley Forge, which invokes the spirit of George Washington, who had nothing but contempt for wise guys.

EDDIE: Oh Jesus, Pop.

HARVEY: And don't swear, please. *(More affectionately; going to him)* Oh now look, Eddie. You're a good boy at heart. I'm convinced of that. Bishop Davis told me that in confirmation classes, you exhibited a sensitive soul.

EDDIE: I did not!

HARVEY: He says you did, and he's a bishop! So all I ask is that you remember that whatever you say or do—whether it be an unattractive remark or an unsuitable deed—it will affect the lives of not only me and your mother, and your sister and brother, but also your grandparents on both sides, and my three brothers, and your several aunts, let alone Miss Bacon, and Charlie, and—

*(*JANE *returns.)*

JANE: Soup's on.

HARVEY: We'll be right there, darling.

JANE: Oh, and that was your mother on the telephone....

HARVEY: What? Is she all right?

JANE: Of course she's all right. But she wants to see Eddie.

EDDIE: Why?

JANE: She didn't say.

HARVEY: Did she mention anything about school?

JANE: She did not. *(She goes off.)*

HARVEY: You'd better go see her..

EDDIE: Now?

HARVEY: No not now, obviously. It's dinner time now. Go see her this Saturday afternoon, when she is less likely to bring up things like work and school.

EDDIE: O K.

HARVEY: And if she does, you're doing Independent Study, remember.

EDDIE: I know, Pop.

HARVEY: All right then. Now go tell your brother and sister it's dinner time. And wash your hands. And start thinking about how to avoid ruining your life, and embarrassing your family, and killing your grandmother.

(He goes off, as ANNIE*, a maid, comes on.)*

ANNIE: *(Irish accent)* Your grandmother's lying down, Mister Eddie.

EDDIE: She lies down a lot, doesn't she?.

ANNIE: Ah well, she has her heart.

EDDIE: I'll wait then, Annie.

*(*ANNIE *goes.)*

EDDIE: *(To audience)* I'll bet you think this is sort of a drag, having to visit my grandmother on a Saturday afternoon, when they've just finished shaving the ice on Delaware Park Lake, and I could be playing shinny hockey on black ice with the whole gang. But I have to admit I kind of like visiting her. She always makes me feel good, my grandmother. She never criticizes or makes me feel shittier than I sometimes do already. My mother says she has a mean streak in her, but I've never seen it. And my grandmother's never seen mine, either. But even if she did, we still might get along. For example, if I told her that I had just murdered someone, she'd say, "I'm sure you did what was best, Eddie dear." And if I told her I was going to jail, she'd say, "I hope you meet nice new friends." That's how it is with my grandmother .Of course how she'd go for the fact I'm a pervert who draws dirty pictures is another matter.

(ANNIE *comes back in.)*

ANNIE: Your grandmother's getting up, Mister Eddie.. *(She takes a chair and starts off with it.)*

EDDIE: What are you doing, Annie?

ANNIE: I'm putting her chair on the staircase landing. She likes to sit and rest on her way up and down.

EDDIE: Because of her heart?

ANNIE: Because of her heart... Oh and did you notice them nice roses on the hall table, Mister Eddie?

EDDIE: *(Looking off)* Oh yeah.

ANNIE: Mister Lambert brought her those.

EDDIE: What? Lambert was here?

ANNIE: He stopped by this morning. Second time this week. He and your grandmother have nice chats. *(She goes.)*

EDDIE: *(To audience)* See? See what he does, that slimy bastard? Roses this time. Always trying to get in good with people. Last Christmas he gave my grandfather special tobacco for his pipe, when I forgot to give him anything at all. Oh I'm telling you, that Lambert makes my Indian blood boil.

GRANDMOTHER: *(From off)* Is that you, Eddie?

EDDIE: It's me all right.

GRANDMOTHER: *(From off)* I'll be right down, dear. Let me just sit a moment and catch my breath.

EDDIE: Do you feel O K?

GRANDMOTHER: *(From off)* Oh yes. It's just my heart.

EDDIE: Take your time, Gog. *(To audience)* Notice that I call her Gog. All the grandchildren do. When you write her a thank-you note, you spell it G-O-G. Gog. My mother says that's what the Philistines in the Bible called their false idols— "They fell down and worshipped before the altars of Gog". Yeah well, lots of people have sappy names for their grandmothers.

GRANDMOTHER: *(Coming in, helped by* ANNIE*)* I have to take my time, dear boy. Apparently I have too big heart. *(Kisses him)* How lovely to see you, dear boy.

EDDIE: You smell good, Gog.

GRANDMOTHER: That's because your father and his brothers always give me special soap from Saks Fifth Avenue for my birthday.

EDDIE: *(To audience)* And she has such soft skin. My mother says it's because she never lifts a finger.

*(*ANNIE *sets up her chair.)*

GRANDMOTHER: Annie, please bring this dear, sweet boy a big glass of ginger ale and a plate of Nelly's nice sugar cookies.

ANNIE: Yes, Missus... *(As she goes off, she sneezes.)*

GRANDMOTHER: *(Low, to* EDDIE*)* Did you hear that?

EDDIE: Hear what?

GRANDMOTHER: That noise she made.

EDDIE: She just sneezed, that's all, Gog.

GRANDMOTHER: She doesn't have to sneeze.

EDDIE: Maybe she's got a cold.

GRANDMOTHER: She doesn't have to get a cold. She does it just to annoy me. *(Produces a key)* Now Eddie, take this key, go to my desk, unlock the third drawer, and you'll find a little surprise.

EDDIE: Candy? *(To audience)* Per usual..

GRANDMOTHER: Delicious licorice drops from Fannie Farmer's. Take one for yourself and bring one to me, and hide the key under the ink bottle..

EDDIE: O K, Gog. *(As he gets the candy)* How come you always lock up your candy, Gog?

GRANDMOTHER: Because the maids steal it.

EDDIE: *(To audience)* My mother says the maids don't steal a thing. Gog runs them so hard the poor things don't have time.

(He and his GRANDMOTHER *share the candy.)*

GRANDMOTHER: Tell me about your life, Eddie dear. Do you have nice friends? Do you play nice games? Are you learning exciting things at school?

EDDIE: *(To audience)* So I told her the usual stuff guys tell their grandmothers.

*(*ANNIE *returns with a tray of ginger ale and cookies.)*

EDDIE: Thanks, Annie.

*(*ANNIE *goes;* EDDIE *balances the tray on his knees.)*

GRANDMOTHER: Oh by the way, Eddie. Were you sick this week?

EDDIE: Sick?

GRANDMOTHER: Your cousin Lambert said you haven't been in school the last few days.

EDDIE: *(To audience)* See? Knew it! Lambert doing his dirty work. *(To* GRANDMOTHER*)* No, not really sick, Gog.

GRANDMOTHER: Because if you've been sick, dear boy, I owe you a book. All my grandchildren get books when they're sick. *(Getting up)* I'll telephone the bookstore and ask Mrs Irwin to pick out the latest *Oz* book, and have it delivered immediately..

EDDIE: I'm too old for the Oz books now, Gog.

GRANDMOTHER: *(Kissing him)* Then I'll tell her simply to pick out a good book for a good boy.

EDDIE: *(To audience)* Jeez, I can't stand this. *(To* GRANDMOTHER*)* Actually I haven't been sick, Gog. I've been doing independent study at home.

GRANDMOTHER: Independent study! Why that's wonderful, Eddie! Tell me what you've been studying...

EDDIE: Oh, well. Various things. Art, really. I've been studying art.

GRANDMOTHER: Art! Oh my! You draw so well. I remember once you drew me my own special Valentine.

EDDIE: *(To audience)* That was when I was younger.

GRANDMOTHER: Tell me what you've been drawing this time.

EDDIE: *(To audience)* I couldn't lie. She was so sweet and soft, and smelled so good.. *(To* GRANDMOTHER*)*) Gog, I have to tell you. I'm studying at home because I was suspended from school.

GRANDMOTHER: Suspended? Good gracious, why, dear boy?

EDDIE: Because I wasn't paying attention in Latin class.

GRANDMOTHER: Were you distracted in some way?

EDDIE: Yes I was, Gog. That's it. I was definitely distracted.

GRANDMOTHER: Now that's very strange indeed, because your cousin Lambert told me he was distracted as well. In the very same class.

EDDIE: Did he tell you why?

GRANDMOTHER: No he didn't. He said you might be able to answer that question.

EDDIE: Oh yes?

GRANDMOTHER: *(Settling back into her chair)* You boys must have a very bad Latin teacher if he lets everyone get distracted.

EDDIE: The teacher's not bad, Gog.... It's me that's bad....

GRANDMOTHER: I don't believe that for one minute, Eddie.

EDDIE: I drew a picture in that class. That's what distracted people. *(Praying)* Oh please, please, God, don't let her have a heart attack.

GRANDMOTHER: A picture? What was your picture of, Eddie?

EDDIE: It was a picture...it was a picture of... It was a picture of a man and woman in love. *(To audience, defensively)* Which could be true! Maybe that's why Injun Joe and Glinda the Good were having sex. Because they were in love. That's not lying, is it?

GRANDMOTHER: Love is nothing to be ashamed of, Eddie. We all fall in love. Your grandfather fell in love with me, and on our wedding trip, took me all the way to Bermuda! Are you in love with someone?

EDDIE: Maybe. Sort of.

GRANDMOTHER: Does she have an attractive nose?

EDDIE: I don't know, Gog.

GRANDMOTHER: The nose is important, Eddie. The nose and the chin line. Always keep that in mind.

EDDIE: I will, Gog.

GRANDMOTHER: You yourself have got a lovely nose.

EDDIE: Thank you.

GRANDMOTHER: I imagine twenty girls are in love with you.

EDDIE: Because of my nose?

GRANDMOTHER: Because you're such a bright, dear boy. But I'm upset, Eddie.

EDDIE: Why, Gog?

GRANDMOTHER: I'm upset you'd be punished simply for drawing a romantic picture.

EDDIE: Oh well.

GRANDMOTHER: No, I don't like that at all. When your grandfather comes home from the bank, I intend to ask him to telephone that school, and tell them to take you back immediately.

EDDIE: No, Gog, no!

GRANDMOTHER: I most certainly am. And they'll listen to your grandfather. He gives them money every year.

EDDIE: No, Gog. Please. I was wrong to draw that picture. I should have been concentrating on my Latin. And it doesn't make any difference, anyway, because Christmas vacation starts the week after next. And besides—

HARVEY: *(From off)* Mother?

GRANDMOTHER: Why, here's your father!

EDDIE: *(To audience)* My father stops to see her almost every day

GRANDMOTHER: Help me up, Eddie. I have to get your father the key.

EDDIE: *(Helping her up)* The key to the candy?

GRANDMOTHER: The key to the liquor cabinet, dear boy. Your father likes to make himself a cocktail.

EDDIE: Do you think the maids would steal the liquor, Gog.

GRANDMOTHER: Without question. Mrs Warren's maid stole a bottle of scotch, and the keys to her Packard, and drove all the way to Albany..

(She goes off as EDDIE *and* HARVEY *set up two chairs to serve as a car.)*

EDDIE: *(To audience)* Afterwards, in the car with my father, he gave me a compliment.

HARVEY: Your grandmother said she had a good conversation with you.

EDDIE: That's right.

HARVEY: She said you're becoming interested in art, especially romantic subjects.

EDDIE: Did she?

HARVEY: Sounds like you managed to cover your tracks quite efficiently..

EDDIE: That's an old Indian expression, did you know that, Pop? "Covering your tracks."

HARVEY: I'm not quite as interested in Indians as you are, Eddie.

EDDIE: I know that.

HARVEY: What I *am* interested in is your behavior. And you must have behaved very well. Because your grandmother is now thinking of inviting you to join the grown-ups for the annual Christmas night dinner.

EDDIE: *(To audience)* I have the feeling I'm supposed to jump up and down.

HARVEY: *Thinking* of it, I said. She normally doesn't invite any grandchildren because she thinks that they all should stay home on Christmas night, and play quietly with their doll houses and electric trains. But she may invite you. You're a lucky man.

EDDIE: *(To audience)* And when we got home...

*(*EDDIE *and* HARVEY *leave the car as* JANE *comes on.)*

HARVEY: Hello, darling. *(Kisses her)*

JANE: Guess who just telephoned?

HARVEY: *(Worried)* My mother?

JANE: Your father. *(To* EDDIE*)* Eddie, your grandfather wants to have lunch with you on Monday.

EDDIE: What about?

JANE: He didn't say.

HARVEY: Mother probably just told him about your independent study, and he wants to know more about it.

EDDIE: Uh-oh.

HARVEY: He takes education very seriously, Eddie. Probably because he didn't have much of one himself. You may have to modify what you told your grandmother. *(To* JANE*)* He told Mother he was studying romantic painting.

JANE: You're studying life, Eddie. Tell your grandfather you're studying life.

HARVEY: *(To* JANE*)* Father's discovered Dickens in his old age. *(To* EDDIE*)* Say you're studying Dickens.

EDDIE: Why do I have to lie all the time?

HARVEY: You won't be lying. You can read *Great Expectations* this weekend.

EDDIE: How long is it?

HARVEY: Long enough to keep you out of trouble.

JANE: In any case, Your grandfather wants you to show up at the bank at a quarter to one.

HARVEY: Be sure to wear a necktie, Eddie. And polish your shoes. You can always tell a gentleman by his linen and his leather.

JANE: God help us.

HARVEY: And your grandfather's secretary's name is Mrs Stawicki. Can you remember that?

EDDIE: Mrs Stawicki.

HARVEY: Exactly. She's a Polish lady of ample proportions.

JANE: Her husband plays the viola in the orchestra, actually.

HARVEY: No need to get into that. Just go right up to her desk, look her in the eye, and say "Good Morning, Mrs Stawicki. I'm Eddie and I have a luncheon appointment with my grandfather."

JANE: Say what you feel like saying, Eddie.

HARVEY: You'll probably have lunch right there, because as president of the bank, your grandfather likes to be accessible during banking hours. When he asks you what you'd like, say the chicken sandwich and a banana for dessert.

JANE: Oh Harvey, let the boy breathe, for heaven's sake!

HARVEY: The chicken sandwiches happen to be superb, Jane. He orders them from the old Lafayette Hotel, and they contain all white meat. And bananas are easy to eat.

EDDIE: Can I order a vanilla milkshake?

HARVEY: No, you may not. And when your grandfather speaks to you, Eddie, speak slowly and clearly because he's somewhat deaf in his left ear.

EDDIE: O K, O K.

HARVEY: Now think about it, Eddie. Lunch with your grandfather! And possibly dinner Christmas night with the grown-ups! For a fellow who has just made a major mistake in his life, you seem to be landing on your feet!

EDDIE: *(Dryly)* Yeah yeah

HARVEY: Let's look in the book-case, Jane. Let's see if we can locate that leather-bound copy of *Great Expectations* we inherited from Aunt Esther.

*(*HARVEY *and* JANE *go off, as* EDDIE *comes downstage)*

EDDIE: *(To audience, as the first slide projection of the map of Buffalo comes up behind him. Again, quiet piano chords)* My grandfather helped Buffalo become a thriving metropolis. When he was just starting out, he rented a horse and buggy to look at the farms along the shore of Lake Erie. He decided that the land would be good for building factories. So he borrowed a lot of money and bought the land from the farmers, and sold it to the big steel companies so they could build their plants and send their steel down the Erie Canal. And after that he started his own real estate company, to give my father and his brothers something to do in life.

(Map projection changes to commanding window frames)

EDDIE: And now my grandfather is president of the Buffalo Savings Bank. He taught his sons how to make money and now he's teaching them how to save it.

(GRANDFATHER *comes on.)*

GRANDFATHER:Sit over here by the window, Eddie, so that when you get bored with me, you can look out and watch the activity in the harbor.

EDDIE: O K.

GRANDFATHER: Not so many boats any more, though. A freighter or two from Deluth. to stock up the old grain elevators. But practically nothing goes onto the canal now, either way.

*(*MRS STAWICKI *brings in a tray. She is indeed amply proportioned.)*

GRANDFATHER: Thank you, Mrs Stawicki.

*(*MRS STAWICKI *smiles at* EDDIE *and goes.)*

GRANDFATHER: I hear you're in trouble, Eddie.

EDDIE: I'm doing independent study. I'm studying Dickens. I'm reading *Great Expectations*. It's a fascinating book.

GRANDFATHER: I don't believe you Eddie. You're in trouble. I can smell it a mile away.

EDDIE: You're right, Gramp.

GRANDFATHER: I suppose what's behind it is your Indian blood.

EDDIE: It sure is.

GRANDFATHER: You got that from me, you know. Your Indian blood.

EDDIE: I know

GRANDFATHER: You put your ear to the ground, and heard strange sounds. Am I right, Eddie?

EDDIE: Pretty much, Gramp.

GRANDFATHER: Oh sure. You definitely got that from me. My grandmother was an Indian.

EDDIE: A Seneca, right?

GRANDFATHER: Exactly right.

EDDIE: The Senecas were a very warlike tribe.

GRANDFATHER: That's what they say.

EDDIE: Could you tell me about her?

GRANDFATHER: My Indian grandmother? Didn't I ever do that?

EDDIE: Not really, Gramp...

GRANDFATHER: Then here beginneth the lesson. My grandfather—which means your great, great grandfather—traveled out to Buffalo all the way from Windsor Locks, Connecticut. He set up a farm for himself and his wife down in Cataraugus County.

EDDIE: Where the skiing is now?

GRANDFATHER: Exactly. Where you all now ski. My grandfather's wife's name was Prudence. Ever heard that name for a girl?

EDDIE: No sir.

GRANDFATHER: Well that was her name But Prudence died. Of influenza. So my grandfather had to look around for another wife.. A man needs a wife, Eddie. Especially if he's a farmer. He needs all the help he can get.

EDDIE: I'll bet.

GRANDFATHER: So my grandfather met this Indian maiden selling winter squash at the village market down in Salamanca. Her name was Fabiola.

EDDIE: She was a Seneca squaw?

GRANDFATHER: Don't call Indian women squaws, Eddie. They think it's demeaning to be called squaws.

EDDIE: O K.

GRANDFATHER: So my grandfather married this Fabiola and together they produced my father, along with seven other children.

EDDIE: You told me that part.

GRANDFATHER: Did I tell you what joy she brought to his life? He kept a journal and wrote in it every night. Wrote by candlelight. Wrote the following words: "My wife has brought tremendous joy into my life." He never wrote that about Prudence.

EDDIE: We studied Pocahontas in third grade.

GRANDFATHER: Ah hah. There's another Indian lady who saved the day. It's not a bad thing, having Indian blood, Eddie. It comes in handy sometimes.

EDDIE: I agree.

GRANDFATHER: When we feel strongly about things, when we get angry or excited or passionate or sometimes even gloomy about things, we can blame it on our Indian blood. Right?

EDDIE: Right, Gramp.

GRANDFATHER: But it also can bring tremendous joy, Eddie. Remember that. I'm glad I have Indian blood.

EDDIE: So am I, Gramp!

GRANDFATHER: Good boy.

(They settle in to eat.)

EDDIE: Does Lambert have Indian blood?

GRANDFATHER: Your cousin Lambert? Yes he does, but it's a different thing.

EDDIE: He has Tuscarora blood while you and I are Senecas, right?.

GRANDFATHER: Maybe.

EDDIE: The Senecas and Tuscaroras don't get along, right? They have very different customs. I read in a book that the Tuscaroras always wanted to sneak into the stockade, and the Senecas always wanted to get out.

GRANDFATHER: Like Lambert and you, eh?

EDDIE: That's why we don't get along..

GRANDFATHER: I'll tell you this. Lambert's grandmother—
your grandmother's sister, your Aunt Minnie—ran off with an Indian when she was very young. He was a handsome fellow, but turned out to be a drinker. So she returned to Buffalo as soon as she could. rought a baby with her—Lambert's dad.... She doesn't like to talk about all that. She's ashamed of her Indian connection. And so is Lambert.

EDDIE: I'm proud of mine.

GRANDFATHER: So am I, but keep an eye on it, Eddie. It can get you into serious trouble.

EDDIE: Did it ever get you into trouble, Gramp?

GRANDFATHER: Twice in my life. The first time I'll you about if I'm still alive when you're twenty-one. The second time I'll tell you about right now. I became too fond of cocktails, Eddie.

EDDIE: The old fire-water?

GRANDFATHER: Exactly. The old fire-water. So I gave it up, Eddie.

(MRS STAWICKI *comes in, carrying his overcoat, hat and scarf, leaving them on a chair.)*

MRS STAWICKI: You've got a board meeting in ten minutes, sir. Over at the Bethlehem Steel offices.

GRANDFATHER: Thank you, Mrs Stawicki.

(MRS STAWICKI *clears off the tray, again smiles at* EDDIE, *and exits.)*

GRANDFATHER: Your grandmother wants me to call the school and get you reinstated immediately. Do you want me to do that?

EDDIE: You don't have to, Gramp..

GRANDFATHER: I know I don't have to. Do you want me to?

EDDIE: No, Gramp.

GRANDFATHER: Didn't think so.

(EDDIE *helps him put on his overcoat.)*

GRANDFATHER: Your grandmother feels you're being punished because of your artistic talents. Is that true?

EDDIE: Sort of.

GRANDFATHER: You think you have artistic talent?

EDDIE: Sometimes maybe. A little.

GRANDFATHER: Suppose I tell her the artist is often misunderstood.

EDDIE: O K.

GRANDFATHER: Suppose I say that the artist often suffers at the hands of society. And he has to learn to live with this. And sometimes it improves his art.

EDDIE: That's good, Gramp. Tell her that.

GRANDFATHER: We tell a lot of lies in life, don't we, Eddie?

EDDIE: Yes sir, we do.

GRANDFATHER: Sometimes we have to. To keep the ball rolling.

EDDIE: Yes sir.

GRANDFATHER: *(To* EDDIE*; handing him a bill)* Here's five dollars, Eddie. Your grandmother tells me you have a girl.

EDDIE: Sort of, Gramp. Not really.

GRANDFATHER: Does she like gardenias?

EDDIE: I don't know, Gramp.

GRANDFATHER: Send her a gardenia. If she likes it, she'll let you know. Then your Indian blood will come in very handy. *(He goes.)*

(Sound of Christmas carols, as if on the radio)

*(*JANE *comes on.)*

JANE: *(Setting up a chair)* Want to help me with the Christmas tree ornaments, Eddie?

EDDIE: Sure. *(He helps her onto a chair, hands her ornaments)*

JANE: Are you ready to make unto the Lord a joyful noise?

EDDIE: Why should I?

JANE: You've been invited to your grandmother's Christmas night.

EDDIE: What's so great about that?

JANE: Nothing. But I happen to be married to someone who might disagree. You can always say you've got other plans.

EDDIE: I was planning to go to the movies Christmas night with Bucky Zeller.

JANE: What movie?

EDDIE: *Abbott and Costello Meet Frankenstein.*

JANE: I almost wish I could go with you.

EDDIE: You can, Mom. If you pay and don't sit near us.

JANE: Better not, Eddie.

EDDIE: Why don't you want to go to Gog's?

JANE: Lots of reasons. For one thing the food is horrible.

EDDIE: You don't think Nelly is a good cook?

JANE: I think poor Nelly never gets the chance. During the war, when our Agnes left to work for Bell Aircraft, and I had to learn to cook, I discovered that a lot of good food depends on onions and garlic. And Nelly doesn't use them.

EDDIE: Why not?

JANE: Your grandmother won't have them in the house. She thinks that only immigrants cook with onions and garlic.

EDDIE: Can't Nelly sneak them in?

JANE: She doesn't dare. Wait till you taste the stuffing for the turkey.

EDDIE: I love stuffing.

JANE: You won't like this. And don't call it "stuffing".Your grandmother thinks the word is vulgar. You have to call it "dressing".

EDDIE: Dressing.

JANE: That's it, and say it's absolutely delicious.

EDDIE: But it isn't?

JANE: It's nothing crumbled up, soggy white bread. And poor Nelly is thoroughly embarrassed about it.

EDDIE: You're kind of steamed up, aren't you, Mom?

JANE: I suppose I am. It's all too much! Did you know that when your father and I were first married, we had to go eat at your grandmother's every Wednesday and Sunday night! Rain or shine. Plus Thanksgiving. Plus Christmas. Plus Easter. Plus her two birthdays.

EDDIE: What two birthdays?

JANE: You haven't noticed that she has two birthdays? There's the real one in October. But she thinks it's depressing to have been born in the fall. So she celebrates another on the first of May. And woe unto those who forget either.

EDDIE: She gets presents both times?

JANE: You bet. And they'd better be good ones.

EDDIE: Smart lady.

JANE: Do you know how I finally got out of going there every other minute?

EDDIE: How?

JANE: Never mind. I shouldn't tell you this.

EDDIE: How, Mom?

JANE: Oh hell You're old enough. One Sunday night, as we were getting ready to go, and your father was saying I had put on too much lipstick, I simply lay down on the floor and started kicking and screaming.

EDDIE: Mom!

JANE: I did. And then I got up and threw a clothes brush at him..

EDDIE: Did you hit him?.

JANE: On the head. I behaved like a candidate for the loony bin. But you know something? All the time I was doing it, it felt absolutely wonderful.

EDDIE: Maybe you've got Indian blood, too.

JANE: I don't know what I've got. But I'll tell you one thing: ever since I did that, your father has agreed to stay home every Sunday night and listen to Jack Benny on the radio.

EDDIE: Good for you, Mom.

JANE: Well it was a major step for me. And more of a step for him. He's always had a hard time leaving home. When we were first married, we had to live right around the corner from his mother. And it took him two years before he stopped sneaking over to use the bathroom.

EDDIE: Oh my God. *(Taking another ornament out of the box)* Do you still want to hang this thing I made in second grade?

JANE: *(Giving hm a quick kiss)* Of course. It wouldn't be Christmas without it ...

(Moves the chair. EDDIE *helps her up again)*

JANE: Anyway, the spotlight's on you, kiddo, Christmas night. Your grandmother has given you a special dispensation, over all her other grandchildren. You must have made a big hit with your independent study.

EDDIE: I guess I did.

JANE: There might be another reason, too.

EDDIE: What's that?

JANE: She wants you to be company for Lambert.

EDDIE: What?

JANE: Lambert will be there, too.

EDDIE: Why, for God's sake?

JANE: Apparently the poor boy has no place else to go. His father has long since vamoosed out of the picture, and his mother has decided to spend Christmas with some shoe salesman in Rochester. So he's stuck with his grandmother, your great Aunt Minnie, and your grandmother's stuck with both.

EDDIE: What about Grandpa? Does he like Lambert?

JANE: He pays for his education, I can tell you that. And supports Aunt Minnie, too. Poor thing hasn't got a nickel.

EDDIE: I didn't know that.

JANE: Don't you breathe a word of this, by the way.... You'd embarrass everyone involved.

EDDIE: I promise I won't, Mom.

JANE: Your grandfather is a dear and generous man.

EDDIE: He's where I got my Indian blood.

JANE: Well don't bring that up with your father.

EDDIE: But now I'm worried about Christmas night. It makes me act up when I'm around Lambert.

JANE: Just make a concerted effort. Grin and bear it. Which is what I do when I'm there. *(Pause)* And here, too, sometimes, as a matter of fact... *(She goes off.)*

EDDIE: *(To audience)* My mother likes to be alone sometimes. For example, on Saturday afternoons, she always listens to the opera, while my father plays gin-rummy down at his club. And me? I go to the movies with my friends. Or to plays, sometimes, with my grandmother. Once she took me to a play at the Erlanger theatre where you could see snow coming down outside a window of a log cabin. It looked really neat. I told my English teacher about it and he said that they had a play in New York called *Our Town* which had hardly any scenery at all. The movies are the place to show snow, he said, and plays should require us to use our imaginations. Well, in Buffalo, we usually have a major snowstorm around Christmastime, so because this is a play, you'll just have to imagine what it was like.

(EDDIE *goes off, as* HARVEY *and* JANE *come on, wearing overcoats and golashes. They set up two chairs for the front seat of a car.* HARVEY *honks the horn.)*

HARVEY: Where is that boy?

JANE: I think he's on the telephone.

HARVEY: On the telephone? On Christmas night?

JANE: I think he's talking to one of the Nussbaumer girls.

HARVEY: He's interested in girls now?

JANE: At least in little Peggy Nussbaumer.

HARVEY: And she's interested in him?

JANE: She telephoned, at least.

(HARVEY *honks the horn again.)*

HARVEY: Is Peggy Nussbaumer a Jewess?

JANE: Harvey!

HARVEY: Calling on Christmas night.

JANE: I don't know whether she is or not.

HARVEY: She may easily be a Jewess.

JANE: Harvey! Stop saying that!. You can't say Jewess or Negress or any of those things any more.

HARVEY: Why not?

JANE: You just can't. Peach Taylor doesn't even like being called a sculptress.

HARVEY: May I say foolish-ness?

JANE: If I can say preju-dess..

HARVEY: I thought there was freedom of speech in this country.

*(*HARVEY *hits the horn again.* EDDIE *comes on, now in overcoat, hat and golashes. He kneels behind them, as if he were in the back seat.)*

EDDIE: Sorry.

HARVEY: Did you have a pleasant conversation?

EDDIE: It was O K.

HARVEY: Did you convey our regards to her parents?

EDDIE: No.

HARVEY: Next time, do it, please.

EDDIE: Even on the telephone?

HARVEY: Especially on the telephone, even though it is a frustrating and inadequate instrument. Someday, when you're older, after talking to a girl, you'll put it down and say to yourself, "I need more than a disembodied voice. I need to see the light in her eyes and the smile on her face." That's what I say to myself whenever I telephone your mother.

JANE: I'm not always smiling, I can tell you that....

HARVEY: Never mind. I say it anyway. And you'll say it, too, Eddie, when you fall in love.

EDDIE: Let's not talk about it, huh?

HARVEY: Are we now saying "Huh"?

JANE: *(Dryly)* I thought there was freedom of speech in this country.

HARVEY: I don't consider "huh" to be speech, Jane. I suspect that Neanderthal cavemen lurched around the jungle saying "huh." long before language was invented. ...Now let me focus on my driving, in view of all this snow....

(Sound of windshield wipers, tire chains, occasional gusts of wind)

HARVEY: By the way, Eddie, I had Vito, the furnace man, put chains on the tires. Just to be on the safe side.

EDDIE: I hear them.

HARVEY: And I gave him an extra five dollars for doing it. Which means when we get back, he will also have shoveled the front walk. So you're off the hook. Merry Christmas.

EDDIE: Thanks, Pop. *(Looking out; stands up, speaks to audience)* It's quite a storm out there. You'll have to imagine us driving through the Park, and seeing snow on the head and shoulders and fig-leaf of the statue of David, by Michaelangelo, which is an exact copy of the one in Florence, Italy. Except for the fig-leaf, which we added in Buffalo. And you'll have to imagine snow bending down the branches of the American elms as we drove down Delaware Avenue toward my grandmother's.

JANE: *(Looking out)* They're dying, you know.

EDDIE: *(Again kneeling behind)* Who's dying?

JANE: The elms. I read somewhere that some bug is getting under their bark and killing them, bit by bit.

HARVEY: They'll find a cure. They always do.

JANE: Oh let's hope. They're so beautiful. And so are these lovely old houses. And everything looks even lovelier in the snow. I don't know why people criticize our weather. The snow makes the whole world look special.

HARVEY: Which is why we appreciate our winters, Eddie.

JANE: We take advantage of it. We ski, we toboggan, we skate....

EDDIE: The Larkins have built a big toboggan slide right in their back yard.

HARVEY: There you are.

(They drive. EDDIE *takes out a pack of gum, opens it, chews noisily.)*

HARVEY: Oh good God..

JANE: Now what?

HARVEY: I believe I detect the sound of someone chewing gum.

JANE: It was in his stocking, Harvey.

HARVEY: You'd think Santa Claus might have been a bit more imaginative... Spit it out, please, Eddie.

EDDIE: I just put it in.

HARVEY: Spit it out, please. Are we becoming ruminants now? Are we committed to chewing the cud?

JANE: Oh Harvey.

HARVEY: I don't want my dear mother to see a child of mine chewing gum.

JANE: Nonsense. She chews it herself occasionally.

HARVEY: She does not!

JANE: I specifically heard your brother Paul say that he and your mother sometimes share a stick of Beeman's before going to bed.

HARVEY: That would be upstairs, Jane. At night. With the shades down. So it doesn't count. *(To* EDDIE*)* Spit out your gum, Eddie. And fold it neatly into its wrapper so you don't make life more difficult for everyone else in the world.

JANE: Hand it to me, Eddie. I'll stick it in the ashtray.

(EDDIE *does)*

EDDIE: Do you think Uncle Paul will ever get married?

HARVEY: *(Quickly)* No.

JANE: He's a confirmed bachelor, Eddie..

EDDIE: Why?

HARVEY: Why? Why? Because he wants to be, that's why.

JANE: Because different people lead different lives, Eddie.

HARVEY: I'll give you a better answer than that, Eddie. Your Uncle Paul has never married because life is so pleasant living with your grandmother that he sees no reason to leave.

JANE: You sound a little envious.

HARVEY: Never, darling! My life began when I married you.... Or at least a different life.

JANE: I should hope so

EDDIE: Who else will be there? Besides Lambert, I mean. And his grandmother..

HARVEY: Your grandparents, of course. And your uncles and aunts. And Professor Levy from the University, who specializes in Victorian Literature.

JANE: Thank God for Professor Levy. At least he leavens the lump.

HARVEY: Lump? What lump?

JANE: *(Looking out the window)* Never mind.

HARVEY: Professor Levy is Jewish, Eddie, and your grandmother invites him every year because the Jews have nothing to do on Christmas....

JANE: I'm amazed he keeps coming.

HARVEY: He keeps coming, Jane, to bask in the warmth of American family life.

JANE: You may be right. Since the Germans deprived him of most of his own.

HARVEY: Exactly.

JANE: Sometimes I think he's there because we amuse him.

HARVEY: Amuse him, Jane? Amuse him?

JANE: We all must seem very silly and peculiar.

HARVEY: I won't dignify that comment with a response.

EDDIE: *(Standing up; to audience)* And so we got to my grandmother's.. And in Buffalo, in the winter, there's a lot of fussing with coats and overshoes ...

*(*ANNIE *the maid comes out to help* EDDIE, JANE *and* HARVEY *take off their stuff. They load up* ANNIE.*)*

JANE: Merry Christmas, Annie.

ANNIE: Thank you for your Christmas gift, missus. I needed them stockings bad.

JANE: They're nylons, Annie. We can get them again now the war is over.

HARVEY: *(Giving her a bill)* Here's my present for you, Annie. And don't give it to your priest! Go out and have yourself a rip-roaring good time!

ANNIE: Oh, sir...

HARVEY: And tell Nelly and Jean I'll stop by the kitchen later. Is Ralph there?

EDDIE: *(To audience, as they continue to hand* ANNIE *their coats)* Ralph is the chauffeur. My grandparents have this big, beautiful twelve-cylinder Pierce Arrow limousine, made right here in Buffalo, but they don't even know how to drive it. And don't even *want* to. So Ralph drives it for them,

ANNIE: Ralph's having a cup a tea, Mr. Harvey.

HARVEY: *(Piling overcoats on her)* Then I'll be out soon.. And I want all four of you to spend New Year's Eve dancing an Irish jig down at the Town Casino!

ANNIE: *(Giggling)* Oh, sir. Oh sir. *(She goes off laden with winter things)*

JANE: *(Low to* HARVEY*)* I'll bet your mother won't let the poor things out of the house for New Year's Eve.

HARVEY: I was joking with them, Jane. Obviously. I was just spreading a little Christmas cheer.

*(*UNCLE PAUL *comes on)*

PAUL: Welcome. Welcome all.

HARVEY: Here's your Uncle Paul, Eddie, looking sleek as a seal and rich as a Rockefeller from his wise investments.

PAUL: Tip me hello, Eddie.

EDDIE: *(Shaking hands)* Hello, Uncle Paul.

PAUL: Come in, come in.

(They circle into the living room.)

EDDIE: *(Looking around)* Hey! I don't see a Christmas tree.

PAUL: Your grandmother decided not to have one this year. Because of her heart.

HARVEY: Christmas trees take a lot of fussing, Eddie.

JANE: *(To* PAUL*)* So where is Queen Victoria?

PAUL: Tipping her presents in the music room.

HARVEY: I'll tip her hello.

*(*HARVEY *and* PAUL *go off)*

EDDIE: *(To audience)* Maybe you've noticed that my father and his brother use the word "tip" all the time. *(To* JANE*)* What does that actually mean. Mom? The word "tip".

JANE: It means whatever they want it to mean. They used it when they were children, and never stopped.... I'd better go tip her, too, or I'll be thoroughly tipped by your father, after we tip home. *(She goes off.)*

EDDIE: *(As he arranges furniture)* And here's another place in this play where you have to imagine things—in this case, a big room with a fireplace, with a fire in it. But not even a wood fire. Oh no. Just a gas jet, with a log in front of it, not even burning, because my grandmother thinks wood fires are messy and dangerous. You should imagine the furniture, and the piano in the corner, and my Uncle Paul's old cello, which is never used. And you also have to imagine a whole bunch of people sitting around—people you'll never see because crowd scenes belong in Hollywood movies where they have more money. So here's who you won't see: my father's two other brothers, and their wives, and Professor Levy from the University, and my great Aunt Minnie, who ran off with the Indian.

*(*LAMBERT *comes out, with his grandmother on his arm)*

And lo and behold, her grandson, Lambert. Look at him, sitting next to her. He's pretending to listen to her, but notice how sometimes he glances furtively at me.

*(*LAMBERT *glances at him)*

Oh, I hear distant drums here tonight. The Tuscaroras are restless, no doubt about that.

*(*GRANDMOTHER, GRANDFATHER, HARVEY, JANE, *and* PAUL *come on.)*

GRANDMOTHER: *(Kissing* EDDIE*)* Merry Christmas, Eddie. I was just showing everyone my presents..

EDDIE: What did you get this year, Gog?

GRANDMOTHER: A lovely box of soap.

EDDIE: *(Low to* JANE*)* I thought you gave her that for her birthday.

JANE: *(Low to* EDDIE*)* We gave her that for both birthdays.

GRANDMOTHER: And Professor Levy here brought me some sweet-smelling lavender sachet for my drawers.

EDDIE: *(Low to* JANE*)* Her drawers?

JANE: *(Low to* EDDIE*)* Her bureau drawers, Eddie.

EDDIE: Oh.

PAUL: I always give mother jewelry.

GRANDMOTHER: You most certainly do, Paul dear. *(To others)* This year Paul gave me this lovely ruby ring from Jaffe's, which I shall wear till the day I die. *(She shows it around.)*

GRANDFATHER: Now don't say "Merry Christmas" to Professor Levy here, Eddie. He doesn't believe a word of this stuff..

HARVEY: He does when he's here, Father.

GRANDFATHER: Does he? I'm not sure I do.

GRANDMOTHER: Oh Charley.

PAUL: *(Looking off)* Ah hah! I see Annie is tipping the ice for our cocktails.

HARVEY: And I hope she'll tip us some of Nellie's toasted cheese crackers to go with it.

PAUL: There's caviar, too. I already tipped some in the kitchen.

HARVEY: Shall we tip ourselves a cocktail, everyone? Shall we gather around the sacred fount?

PAUL: *(Taking* GRANDMOTHER*'s arm)* May I make you a cocktail, Mother?

GRANDMOTHER: Doctor Russell tells me that a small glass of dry sherry may be good for my heart.

HARVEY: Than we'll tip you a sherry, Mother.

GRANDMOTHER: Just one, though. And that goes for everyone else. You can have too much of a good thing, am I right, Minnie? *(To others)* Poor dear Minnie knows from experience just how right I am.

(She goes off, followed by HARVEY *and* PAUL.*)*

EDDIE: *(To audience)* I guess she means Aunt Minnie's husband was a drunk.

GRANDFATHER: *(To* JANE *, as they go off)* The Professor and I have been discussing Dickens.

JANE: I love Dickens.

GRANDFATHER: I'm just discovering him....Your father tells me you're becoming a Dickens expert, Eddie..

EDDIE: We read *A Tale of Two Cities* next year, Gramp.

(LAMBERT *comes up)*

LAMBERT: I'm reading it now. Just to get ahead. I love it.

GRANDFATHER: Good boy. *(He goes off with* JANE.*)*

(Everyone is off by now except LAMBERT *and* EDDIE.*)*

LAMBERT: You could at least be polite and say hello, Eddie.

EDDIE: Oh right. *(Giving* LAMBERT *the Indian sign)* How.

LAMBERT: How what?

EDDIE: "How" happens to be a greeting between Indians, Lambert. As you damn well know.

LAMBERT: I was still thinking about Dickens.

EDDIE: Oh really? *(To audience)* See what a twerp he is? *(To* LAMBERT*)* Maybe you should do some thinking about how you tried to mess me up with my own grandmother.

LAMBERT: By doing what?

EDDIE: Telling her what happened at school, that's what. Thanks a bunch, pal.

LAMBERT: I just said...

EDDIE: I know what you just said. But it didn't work. I'm back in her good graces.

LAMBERT: For now, at least.

(Sounds of party, muted, offstage).

EDDIE: What do you mean by that, Lambert?

LAMBERT: Come into the lavatory. I'll show you something.

EDDIE: What've you got?

LAMBERT: That's for me to know, and you to find out.

(He moves to a lighted area downstage. EDDIE *follows.)*

EDDIE: So?

LAMBERT: *(As if locking the door)* Hold your water. Just hold your water. *(Reaches into a pocket, produces a folded piece of paper)* How about this? *(He unfolds it.)* Take a gander.

EDDIE: Oh Jeez! *(To audience)* It's that same damn lousy drawing I did over at the Garver's.. *(To* LAMBERT*)* Ted said he'd put it in the incinerator!

LAMBERT: He forgot to light it..

EDDIE: Which means you stole it. Which means once again that the Tuscaroras are a bunch of thieving rascals and scamps.

LAMBERT: Knock it off!

EDDIE: *(Making a grab for it)* Then give it back.

LAMBERT: *(Holding it away from him)* No...

EDDIE: May I have my own personal property back, please, Lambert.

LAMBERT: No.

EDDIE: I'll give you five dollars for it. *(Takes it out of his pocket, displays it)* Five whole dollars. Which I'll bet you can use, too, because you don't have much money. *(To audience)* And which is a lot of money to spend on a minor work of art.

LAMBERT: This is a valuable masterpiece, Eddie. I'll take twenty.

EDDIE: Twenty *dollars*?

LAMBERT: Two-zero.

EDDIE: You bastard! You know I don't have that much.

*(*EDDIE *makes a grab for the drawing. He and* LAMBERT *get into another fight.* HARVEY *comes in.)*

HARVEY: Boys? *(Looks around, then knocks on the lavatory door)* Boys! What's going on in there?

LAMBERT: *(Now in* EDDIE*'s hammerlock)* Eddie spilled something on his pants and I'm helping him clean up.

EDDIE: *(To audience)* See what a natural liar he is!

HARVEY: Well make it snappy, you two, because we're about to go in to dinner. *(He goes off.)*

EDDIE: O K, Lambert. If you show that around to anyone, I'll just say I didn't draw it. Sometimes you have to lie just to keep the ball rolling.

LAMBERT: *(Looking at drawing)* Yeah well, I notice your name on this, Eddie! I see your own personal signature.

EDDIE: Oh shit! *(To audience)* This is what I get for being too conceited and putting my name on a crumby work of art.. .. *(To* LAMBERT*)* Lambert, my friend, let me tell you something, man to man. If you don't watch out, you'll grow up to be the black sheep of this entire family.

LAMBERT: You think so, Eddie?.

EDDIE: I know so, pal.

LAMBERT: Yes, well, I'm going to hold onto this drawing, Eddie. So you better be nice to me tonight. And nice to me at school, too. I want to go with the gang more. When you all go to New Skateland or Crystal Beach, I want you to ask me along. And I want you to invite me for dinner so I can talk to your dad about Yale. Otherwise I'll show this around. And I don't mean just at school, either. I'll make copies of it down at the blueprint place . And I'll mail one to your parents. And another to Peggy Nussbaumer. And I'll even mail one to your grandmother.

EDDIE: That would kill her, you prick! She's got a bad heart.

LAMBERT: Then change your attitude, Eddie!

EDDIE: You know what you're doing, Lambert. You're doing blackmail! Men have died for doing that. And women, too.

HARVEY: *(Coming on)* Come on, boys! Immediately! *(He goes.)*

LAMBERT: *(quickly pocketing the drawing)* Just remember the party isn't over yet, Injun Joe.

(They come out of the lavatory as the lights come up on the rest of the stage. The OTHERS enter as if on their way to dinner, setting up the chairs for the table as they come)

GRANDMOTHER: *(To* GRANDFATHER *as they cross.)* Charley: this summer I want to go to Saranac Lake. I can't stay in Buffalo in August. I get rose fever

GRANDFATHER: It's hay fever, isn't it?

GRANDMOTHER: No, it is not. Farmers get hay fever because they're around hay. I get rose fever because I'm around roses.. *(Calling to Aunt Minnie)* I hope you'll join us at Saranac, Minnie dear.

GRANDFATHER: Who else will be joining this expedition?

GRANDMOTHER: Only Annie, of course.

GRANDFATHER: Ah.. To bring along our sheets. *(To others)* She has to sleep on her own sheets....

GRANDMOTHER: I certainly don't intend to sleep on anyone else's.

(They now circle around as if there were a dining room table, arranging chairs and adlibbing delight about the silver and flowers.)

GRANDMOTHER: Eddie, dear, I want you to sit next to me.

HARVEY: Pull out your grandmother's chair, Eddie

(EDDIE *pulls out her chair for her.)*

GRANDMOTHER: Thank you, dear.

HARVEY: Now push her in. Very gently.

(EDDIE *pushes her in.)*

HARVEY: Good work, Eddie.

GRANDMOTHER: And Lambert, you sit next to my dear sister Annie.

HARVEY: Do the same with *your* grandmother's chair, Lambert. ...

*(*LAMBERT *pushes a chair in elegantly.)*

HARVEY: Very good, Lambert! Excellent!

GRANDMOTHER: Everyone else take your usual seats....

GRANDFATHER: I want to sit next to my friend Jane. *(He does.)*

GRANDMOTHER: Paul, dear, take your father's place at the head of the table.

(They settle in and begin to eat.)

HARVEY: *(Noticing the food)* I'm glad you're serving the family canape, Mother.

GRANDMOTHER: I shall serve it till the day I die.

JANE: *(Low, to* GRANDFATHER*)* Or rather till Nelly dies.

GRANDFATHER: You said it, Jane.

HARVEY: Aren't we having wine this year, Father?

PAUL: Mother won't allow it.

HARVEY: Why no wine, Mother?

GRANDMOTHER: I see no reason to have wine, dear. Everyone's had one cocktail, and that's more than enough alcohol for anyone.

PAUL: The good French wines are beginning to arrive in New York again, Mother.

GRANDMOTHER: Well let's hope they never get to Buffalo.... I worry about wine. And I worry about the French.

HARVEY: Why, Mother?

GRANDMOTHER: Because they drink much too much of it. That's why they keep getting into difficulty with the Germans, who only drink beer.

EDDIE: You mean the war, Gog?

HARVEY: *(Under his breath)* Quiet, Eddie. Don't bring up the war. Her heart, boy! Her heart!

*(*ANNIE *brings in a large platter which is too heavy for her.)*

GRANDMOTHER: Oh look! Here comes the turkey

(The usual ooh's and ah's)

GRANDMOTHER: Nelly carved it in the kitchen so we can all just help ourselves..

*(*ANNIE *has a tough time because when she serves, she has lean over and balance the platter using primarily use one hand.)*

EDDIE: Golly!

GRANDMOTHER: What's the matter, dear?

EDDIE: That platter. It must be hugely heavy.

GRANDMOTHER: It's a solid silver serving platter from Tiffany's, Eddie. It was a wedding present from old Mrs Pommeroy..

EDDIE: Yeah, but gee whiz. *(To* ANNIE*)* Annie? Is that too heavy for you?

HARVEY: Don't speak to Annie while she's working, Eddie.

EDDIE: *(Low to* HARVEY*)* But look what's she's doing. Balancing that whole thing, loaded with turkey and stuffing!

GRANDMOTHER: It's dressing, dear.

EDDIE: But she has to hold it out over the table, with only one hand. And with people pressing down on the plate to snag a good piece. That takes major muscles, Annie!

GRANDMOTHER: Hush, dear.

EDDIE: *(Getting up)* But I could help her, easily. I did seventeen push-ups at school. *(To* ANNIE*)* I'll do that, Annie, and you pass the peas.

JANE: I'll deal with the cranberry, Annie.

HARVEY: Sit down, Eddie!

GRANDMOTHER: Yes, Eddie, dear. Please sit *(Low to him)* You'll hurt Annie's feelings, dear. She'll think she's doing it wrong.

EDDIE: But you need huge biceps.

HARVEY: Just leave it, Eddie. Leave it alone.

*(*EDDIE *sits.* ANNIE *continues to pass)*

HARVEY: *(As he helps himself)* I want to make one thing clear to these boys here. If you're going to eat *with* adults, you'll have to eat *like* adults. Which means no gravy pools in the middle of your mashed potatoes. And no pushing your peas onto your forks with your fingers. And no picking up bones, and gnawing on them like the jackals in Kipling's *Jungle Book....*

JANE: Oh Harvey.

HARVEY: You object to good manners, Jane? You are opposed to civilized behavior?

JANE: It's a festive occasion.

HARVEY: I'm sorry. I like to think we've progressed beyond animals and Hottentots.... Do you agree, Mother?

GRANDMOTHER: I most certainly do.

GRANDFATHER: I don't.

HARVEY: Father, really. I like to think that we are cultivated human beings living in a major city in a powerful country during a crucial century, and this should be most apparent when we sit down to dinner.

GRANDMOTHER: How well you speak, Harvey dear.

GRANDFATHER: You mentioned a major city, Harvey?

EDDIE: We're the thirteenth largest city in the United States.

HARVEY: Quiet, Eddie. The grown-ups are talking.

GRANDFATHER: We were once sixth, Eddie. We were recently thirteenth. But we're not even that any more.

HARVEY: Whatever we are, we're going strong, Father. Things are really humming these days. Our steel mills are operating at full capacity, and we have all those new industries along the Niagara River. There are so many jobs available that the Negroes have arrived in droves from down South., and are making more money than they ever made before.

PAUL: Surely you're pleased, Father.

GRANDFATHER: I'm not at all.

GRANDMOTHER: Your father is Mister Grumpy, boys.... Always is, always has been.

GRANDFATHER: That's because I see around the corner. Oh sure, we're riding high at the moment, because the war is just over. But you boys forget that every major industry here is owned out of town. I had a meeting with the Bethlehem Steel people the other day, and they tell me they're planning to cut production. Their money has never stayed here, and before long, it won't come here either. Am I right, Professor Levy?

(They all look toward the Professor)

You see? The Professor agrees ... Our factories will cut back, and then, you watch: we'll be the first place they'll want to shut down. The railroads have already decided to circumvent us, and the Canadians are talking about a seaway which will bring ships down the Saint Lawrence, across Lake Ontario, and around the Falls through the Welland Canal.. We're being bi-passed, folks, We're obsolete, we're through. You boys can sit in your fancy offices and wave to the trains as they go on to Chicago and to the freighters headed straight on through to Lake Superior.

GRANDMOTHER: I don't understand business. Never have. Never will.

HARVEY: *(reaching across, squeezing her hand)* Thank God you never have to, Mother.

PAUL: I have to admit some people don't like it here. I was in the steam room with Frank Applegate the other day ...

GRANDMOTHER: Paul adores that steam room...

PAUL: The point is Frank announced he was moving to California. "Why, Frank?" I asked. "Why on earth would anyone want to leave Buffalo? And he said it was our weather."

GRANDMOTHER: We have lovely weather.

PAUL: He was thinking of our snow, Mother.

GRANDMOTHER: We have lovely snow.

GRANDFATHER: It's not our snow. It's us.

HARVEY: Us, Father? Us?

GRANDFATHER: We've painted ourselves into a corner.

PAUL: You mean geographically, Father?

GRANDFATHER: I mean much more than that. We don't reach out, boys. Whole new populations arrive on our doorstep, year after year. The Irish, the Italians, the Poles, now the Negroes. Do we connect with them? Do we bring them in? Do we do business with them at any level, unless we have to? Or what about the university? We have a major university sitting out there on Main Street? Do we make use of that illustrious pool of knowledge? Do we ever speak to anyone out there except Professor Levy here? Am I right, Professor?

(Again, they all look toward the Professor.)

GRANDFATHER: The Professor is too polite to criticize his hosts. But I can and will. Because I'm criticizing myself. We huddle in our private schools, and our men's clubs, and our restricted summer communities along the lakeshore, while the city collapses around us.

EDDIE: How can we fix things, Gramp?

HARVEY: Quiet, Eddie. Children should be seen, but not heard.

GRANDFATHER: No, I see him, I hear him, and I'll try to answer him. And the answer is I don't know, Eddie. Maybe it's in the nature of things that if you become successful in life, and make money, and acquire those things you think you want, why maybe you automatically become selfish and snobbish and lose your community spirit. Maybe it's a rule of life. And so—what was that quote you gave me, Professor? The one from Tennyson? No, don't tell me. *(Tapping his forehead)* The library's still here. It just takes the librarian longer to get around... *(He reaches for it.)* "The old order changeth, yielding place to new... Lest... Lest... Lest one good custom should corrupt the world."

EDDIE: What's the one good custom, Gramp?

GRANDFATHER: I suppose it's this. All this. *(Gesturing around)* All of you. The family. But we need new blood around here, Eddie.

EDDIE: Indian blood?

GRANDMOTHER: Oh Eddie, dear, no. I don't like that expression. I never have. It makes me very nervous. *(Whispering)* And look at your poor Aunt Minnie. Whenever you mention the word Indian, she starts shaking like a leaf. *(As if to Professor)* Because she made a mistake in her youth.

GRANDFATHER: I'll tell you this, Eddie. There's an Indian fellow over on the Canadian side of the Falls who wants to start up a gambling casino. Says it will bring them to life down there.

HARVEY: And do we want that here, Father? Do we want gambling dens in Buffalo?

GRANDFATHER: Well it's up to you boys to come up with something else.

PAUL: Easier said than done, Father. *(Getting up; low to* HARVEY*)* I'm going to tip another drink.

HARVEY: *(Furtively)* Tip me one, too, please.

PAUL: Excuse me, Mother. *(He goes.)*

GRANDFATHER: I understand you like the moving pictures, Eddie..

EDDIE: I sure do.

GRANDFATHER: Well the other afternoon, Eddie, I stopped by Shea's Hippodrome to look at the newsreels on the way home. And they showed a Walt Disney cartoon.. They showed a dog chasing a cat. And the cat runs right off a cliff and keeps on running until it looks down. Once it looks down, it falls splat below. Well we're like that cat, Eddie. Sooner or later, we'll look down and see there's nothing underneath us.

HARVEY: Excuse me, Mother.

(He goes off to join PAUL.*)*

GRANDMOTHER: I'd like to change the subject, please.

GRANDFATHER: And what worries me most, Eddie, is that what's true for Buffalo today might be true for this whole darned country tomorrow.

GRANDMOTHER: I want the subject changed, Charlie. Right now.

GRANDFATHER: Yes, yes,, you're right. What's for dessert, Annie?

ANNIE: Vanilla ice cream with chocolate sauce, sir.

GRANDMOTHER: We'll have the fingerbowls first, Annie.

GRANDFATHER: The hell with the fingerbowls! Bring on the ice cream! Am I right, Eddie....

EDDIE: I'll buy that, Gramp....

*(*HARVEY *and* PAUL *return, with their drinks.)*

GRANDMOTHER: Your father is in one of his moods, boys.

*(*HARVEY *and* PAUL *turn their backs and drink simultaneously as* EDDIE *leaves the table and come forward. The lights dim on the others behind him.)*

EDDIE: *(To audience)* All during dinner, in case you didn't notice, I kept sneaking looks at Lambert. And he kept looking back at me. My Indian blood sensed danger. He was just waiting for a time to show that drawing around. If he did, my grandmother would have a heart attack, and my father would send me to military school, and even my mother might give up on me. It's one thing to be suspended from school, but it's much worse to be exiled from your hunting ground. Any Indian can tell you that.

(Everyone gets up from the table.)

GRANDMOTHER: *(Clapping her hands)* Now. Eddie and Lambert, listen to this: it's the custom in this family for everyone to do something entertaining after dinner.

HARVEY: That's true. And it's a great custom, Mother. It's a sign of civilization.

GRANDMOTHER: I want to know who plans to do what.

HARVEY: Let me help you to your chair, Mother.

GRANDMOTHER: ...and I'm not talking about playing cards, either. I understand the younger generation likes to play bridge after dinner.

JANE: I love bridge.

GRANDFATHER: It's a good game, Jane.

GRANDMOTHER: I'm sure it's a very good game. But it does not allow people to express their god-given talents. Everyone in the world should be able to do something after dinner.

PAUL: Otherwise it's not a party, it's simply a meal.

GRANDMOTHER: Well said, Paul dear.

*(*HARVEY *goes to the piano, plays a riff)*

GRANDMOTHER: I wish I could start the ball rolling. I used to sing.... *(Makes an attempt to sing)*
I Dreamt I Dwelt in Marble Halls.
(Interrupts herself) But of course I can't now, because of my heart.

GRANDFATHER: You sang beautifully, dear.

GRANDMOTHER: Thank you, Charley. And you used to do card tricks.

GRANDFATHER: *(Hiking up his sleeves)* I'll do some now in spite of my arthritis.

GRANDMOTHER: No, no. no. It's the turn of the next generation..

HARVEY: Not Eddie and Lambert, Mother. They're a little young.

GRANDMOTHER: You may be right, dear.

LAMBERT: Eddie has a talent for drawing.

EDDIE: And Lambert has a talent for causing trouble.

HARVEY: *(Quickly)* That's enough, boys.

LAMBERT: *(Patting his jacket pocket)* I'm sure there will come a time when we both can express our god-given talents.

HARVEY: Well said, Lambert. Very wise.

EDDIE: *(To audience)* O K, so here's what people did. First Aunt Minnie got up and told some riddles. I won't even tell you what they were, they were all so dumb....

(Everyone pretends to go with her.)

EDDIE: ...but we all pretended we were stumped so she could giggle and give the answers.

(Everyone pretends to be stumped.)

EDDIE: But when she asked. "What's black and white and red all over?" I couldn't help it. I said... *(Shouting it out)* An Indian in a tuxedo!

GRANDMOTHER: No, no, dear. Minnie is a thinking of a newspaper, aren't you, Minnie dear.

HARVEY: *(Low to* EDDIE*)* Apologize. Quickly. Before your Aunt Minnie bursts into tears.

EDDIE: Why? Did her husband wear a tuxedo?

HARVEY: Just do it, Eddie!

EDDIE: Sorry I got it wrong. Aunt Minnie. *(To audience)* So Aunt Minnie just sniffled a little, and sat down.

(Everyone claps.)

EDDIE: Then my two aunts stood up and said they had practiced a little dance, just for the occasion. I wish I could show you this because my Aunt Lily looks like Gene Tierney and my Aunt Martha's a nifty jitterbugger. But that would make this a musical, which means changing everything.

HARVEY: *(At the piano)* I suspect you ladies need a little musical support. And what do you know?. I see the sheet music has been already placed before us.

GRANDMOTHER: Harvey plays beautifully.

HARVEY: *(Playing a few chords)* Ready, ladies? ...Good.

(He plays a very lively swing or jitterbug melody; everyone watches with different reactions. Applause at the end)

GRANDMOTHER: *(Disapprovingly)* Oh my! What a naughty little dance! Where did you learn that?

EDDIE: They said they took a private lesson at the Arthur Murray Dance Studio, down on Chippewa Street, just for tonight.

GRANDMOTHER: Well. I certainly admired your footwork.

(More applause)

EDDIE: Then Professor Levy stood up and recited a poem from *Alice in Wonderland*, by Lewis Carroll. It was about a young man talking to an old man named Father William. "You are old, Father William" he kept saying, and asking questions, and getting nothing but dumb answers. And finally the old man tells the young man to "Be off, or I'll kick you downstairs." It was kind of funny. *(As if to the Professor)* Professor Levy: how come that poem?

LAMBERT: You wanted something else, Eddie? Something from *Tom Sawyer* or the Oz books?

EDDIE: Shut up, Lambert!

GRANDMOTHER: Mercy! We don't use that expression in this family.

HARVEY: *(Who is still at the piano)* Did you hear your grandmother, Eddie?

EDDIE: Sorry, Gog.

HARVEY: Besides, Professor Levy can recite whatever he wants to recite.

EDDIE: *(To audience)* But Professor Levy said I had asked a good question, because *Alice in Wonderland* was really a book for grown-ups. He said it was about how the younger generation is always looking for help from the older generation, and the older generation is always passing on useless information, and is no help at all. The Professor should be here to explain this himself, but... *(Indicating the others)* ...plays are like algebra—you work with what you already have.

HARVEY: *(Hitting a chord on the piano)* Now Jane is going to sing a song..

JANE: Oh no Jane isn't.

HARVEY: It's your turn, darling. And you do it beautifully..

EDDIE: Come on, Mom. *(To audience)* I heard her sing at my father's fiftieth birthday party. She's not as good as the lady on the Hit Parade, but she's not bad, either.

GRANDMOTHER: Do sing, Jane.

GRANDFATHER: For me, Janie. How about it?

JANE: Oh well. You asked for it.

(She joins HARVEY *at the piano.)*

HARVEY: *Why Do I Love You?* from *Showboat*?

JANE: No, not that.

PAUL: Sing *Silent Night.*

GRANDMOTHER: No, dear. That would make the Professor feel uncomfortable.

EDDIE: How about *Indian Love Call*, Mom?

HARVEY: Don't get fresh, Eddie.

JANE: *(To* HARVEY*)* Let's do Cole Porter.

HARVEY: *(To others)* A Yale man, you'll be glad to know. *(To* JANE*) Night and Day* ?

JANE: No, a more recent one...*You'd be So Nice to Come Home to.*

HARVEY: I'll do my best. *(Supporting her with simple chords)*

JANE: *(Tentatively at first, gaining confidence as she goes along)* You'd be so nice to come home to,
You'd be so nice by the fire.
While the breeze on high,
Sings a lullaby,
You'd be all that I
Could desire.

Under stars chilled by the winter,
Under an August moon burning above,
You'd be so nice,
You'd be paradise,
To come home to—and love.

(She ends the song standing behind HARVEY, *who jumps up and kisses her. Everyone applauds.)*

GRANDMOTHER: That was lovely, Jane. But why say he *would* be nice? He *is* nice to come home to, isn't he?

JANE: He will be. Once he decides what's home.

GRANDMOTHER: Well now I want my boys to sing.

HARVEY: I guess it's come to that, my brothers. *(Reaches into his pocket)* And I happen to have tipped along the pitch-pipe

(He blows it. PAUL *joins him in singing a chord)*

HARVEY: Hmmm. *(He gestures as if to the other brothers.)* Gather near, brothers dear. Let's tip it.

GRANDMOTHER: Harvey, dear, I think you boys should do it out in the hall. So Annie and Jean and Nelly can hear while they're putting away the silver.

HARVEY: That's very thoughtful of you, Mother. *(To* PAUL*)* We'll tip it in the hall ...Come on, brothers.

*(*HARVEY *and* PAUL *go off.* GRANDMOTHER, GRANDFATHER, JANE, LAMBERT, *and* EDDIE *remain on stage.)*

GRANDMOTHER: *(To* EDDIE*)* When your father was younger, I had all my boys playing string quartets. Beethoven, Brahms, they each played a different instrument. But now they just like to sing.

(We hear the singers warming up offstage.)

*(*ANNIE *comes in.)*

ANNIE: Ashtrays, Missus?

*(*GRANDMOTHER *puts her finger to her lips.* ANNIE *is stuck on stage. From out and off, we hear the quartet singing. It is good barbershop singing, straightforward and sentimental.)*

QUARTET: *(Offstage)*
Oh Rose, climb up to her window,
And into her casement reach
And say what I may not utter,
In your beautiful, silent speech..."

GRANDFATHER: *(Softly; to* EDDIE*)* Is your grandmother crying yet?...

QUARTET: She will shake the dew from your petals,
She will press you close to her lips,
She will hold you ever so lightly
In her warm white fingertips..."

GRANDMOTHER: *(Softly to* EDDIE*)* They're singing about me, Eddie..

QUARTET: And then, who can tell, she may whisper,
While the city sleeps below,
"I was dreaming of him when you woke me,
But rose, he must never know."

(A long concluding harmonic note. GRANDMOTHER *wipes her eyes and discreetly blows her nose.)*

GRANDMOTHER: Excuse me.

GRANDFATHER: *(Now asleep)* Zzzzz.

(General applause as HARVEY *and* PAUL *come back in)*

GRANDMOTHER: Oh that was so beautiful, my dear, dear boys.

GRANDFATHER: *(Waking up)* Are they going home?

GRANDMOTHER: No, no, Charley. Don't you remember? At the end of the evening, we always play musical chairs. *(To* EDDIE*)* He's getting old and vague. *(To others)* Musical chairs, everyone! ...Professor Levy, I hope you'll join in. ...And Minnie, you, too, dear. And everyone else. Harvey, of course, will play the piano.

*(*PAUL, EDDIE *and* LAMBERT. *quickly set up a circle of three or four chairs.* HARVEY, *at the piano plays a series of brisk, old songs like "Camptown Races", stopping abruptly at certain moments.* EDDIE *and* LAMBERT *circle around the chairs with* JANE *and* PAUL.*)*

EDDIE: *(To audience, as he circles the chairs)* I assume everyone knows how to play this game. You have to imagine everyone playing except my grandparents, Now the deal is that there's always one less chair than there are people, so when the music stops, you have to sit quickly ....

(HARVEY *abruptly stops playing..* EDDIE *sits quickly, as does* LAMBERT; PAUL *is out.)*

EDDIE: ...because if you can't find a chair, you're out of the game. And there's one less chair the next time around.

PAUL *removes a chair; music starts up again)*

EDDIE: So now you have to imagine that Doctor Levy, and my two other uncles, and my two aunts have all been eliminated, one by one ...

(Music stops. JANE *is out, taking a chair with her.)*

EDDIE: Now Mom's out, but Aunt Minnie's still in.

(Music starts up again. EDDIE *and* LAMBERT *are now circling around two chairs. Music stops.* EDDIE *and* LAMBERT *sit quickly.)*

EDDIE: There! See that? No, actually you couldn't, because we don't have enough actors. But if we had an Aunt Minnie here, you would have seen Lambert shove his own *grandmother* out of the way, just to stay in the game!

(EDDIE *removes another chair. Now there's only one left. Music starts again.* EDDIE *and* LAMBERT *start circling quickly)*

EDDIE: So wouldn't you know, it all comes down to Lambert and me.

(HARVEY *now plays very slowly.)*

EDDIE: And now we have to do this in slow motion, like in the movies, so you can get the details of what happens next.

(LAMBERT *and* EDDIE *circle the chair slowly.)*

EDDIE: Because now it all depends on when the music stops. Which means it all depends on my father.

*(*HARVEY *stops his slow playing when* LAMBERT *is in front of the chair.* LAMBERT, *in slow motion starts to sit down.* EDDIE, *in slow motion, pulls the chair out from under* LAMBERT. LAMBERT *falls to the floor.)*

GRANDMOTHER: Oh dear! Oh dear!

(Various gasps from all the others. HARVEY *jumps up from the piano, rushes to* LAMBERT, *helps him up, brushes him off.)*

LAMBERT: *(Holding a handkerchief to his nose, displaying blood)* I've got a bloody nose!

EDDIE: *(To audience)* Only Tuscarora blood, by the way...

GRANDMOTHER: What happened? I'm not sure what happened.

PAUL: Lie down on the floor, Lambert... Put your feet up on a chair.

HARVEY: I apologize for my son, Lambert.

GRANDFATHER: Nobody's hurt, nobody's hurt.

HARVEY: *(To* EDDIE*)* What in heaven's name did you think you were doing?

GRANDFATHER: *(Slyly)* It was your Indian blood, right, Eddie?

EDDIE: You said it, Gramp.

GRANDMOTHER: Oh stop that talk, Charley! I beg you!

HARVEY: I'm waiting for an answer, Eddie.

EDDIE: You rigged that game in favor of Lambert, Pop!

HARVEY: I don't know what you mean?

EDDIE: You stopped the music when he was right in front of the chair!

GRANDMOTHER: I don't like shouting. I won't have it in my house.

HARVEY: *(More quietly)* All right, yes, I did rig the game, Eddie, and you know why?

EDDIE: Why?

HARVEY: Because Lambert isn't as lucky as you are. He doesn't have the benefits of this wonderful family.

EDDIE: What do you mean? He's here, isn't he? He's got Aunt Minnie. And he even got the wishbone from the turkey.

HARVEY: I'm talking about all year long, Eddie. You'll have this family with you for the rest of your life.

JANE: Oh God, I hope not.

HARVEY: Please, Jane. *(To* EDDIE*)* I want you to apologize to Lambert immediately!

GRANDMOTHER: I'm becoming confused. I don't understand what the matter is.

EDDIE: O K, I'll apologize.. *(Goes to where* LAMBERT *is lying on the floor)* Sorry, Lambert. *(Holds out his hand)* Let me help you.

LAMBERT: *(Refusing his help)* Not on your life!

*(*LAMBERT *gets up on his own, walks away from* EDDIE*)*

GRANDMOTHER: Lambert, dear, would you like a nice piece of candy? Paul, get Lambert a piece of candy from my desk.

LAMBERT: I don't want any candy.

PAUL: Did I hear a "no thank you" on that?

LAMBERT: I want something else instead.

GRANDMOTHER: What do you want, dear? Tell us what you want.

LAMBERT: I want Eddie to show us his drawing.

GRANDMOTHER: I don't understand.

LAMBERT: Everyone's been showing off tonight. It's time for Eddie to show off, too.

GRANDFATHER: I think it's time for everyone to go to bed.

LAMBERT: Eddie's such a talented artist. We should see what he can do.

GRANDMOTHER: Would you like to draw us a picture, Eddie.

EDDIE: No thank you, Gog.

LAMBERT: Oh well then. *(Reaching into his pocket)* Eddie doesn't have to draw anything because I happen to have some of his art work right here. *(Takes out the drawing)*

HARVEY: I'd like to see that, please, Lambert.

LAMBERT: I'll just pass it around.

GRANDMOTHER: I'd like to see Eddie's drawing..

HARVEY: Give it to me, please, Lambert. Right now.

*(*LAMBERT *reluctantly hands it to* HARVEY, *who looks at it carefully.)*

EDDIE: *(To audience)* Notice that my father is standing with his back right up to the fireplace so that no one can peek over his shoulder.

(Possibly a red ground light comes up behind HARVEY.*)*

EDDIE: If we had a real fireplace with a real fire in it, all this would be much clearer.

HARVEY: Is this your drawing, Eddie?

EDDIE: Yes, sir.

GRANDMOTHER: I'd like to see the drawing, Harvey.

HARVEY: Would you like your grandmother to see it, Eddie?

EDDIE: No sir.

HARVEY: Would you like your grandfather to see it, Eddie? Or your mother? Or anyone else in this room?

EDDIE: No sir.

HARVEY: Why not, Eddie?

EDDIE: Because it's no good, Pop.

GRANDMOTHER: Nonsense, Eddie. You're a talented boy.

HARVEY: Eddie is speaking of the subject matter, Mother.

EDDIE: No I'm not.

HARVEY: What? You're defending the subject matter?

GRANDMOTHER: Did you draw a romantic picture, Eddie?

HARVEY: Let me handle this please, Mother *(To* EDDIE*)* Why, then, do you think your drawing is no good, Eddie?

EDDIE: Because I did it in a hurry. The hands are wrong.

HARVEY: Much more than that is wrong, my friend.

JANE: Leave it, Harvey. Settle for the hands.

HARVEY: *(After a moment)* I guess I'll have to.... Would you at least agree, Eddie, that there's only one thing to do with this? Namely throw it in the fire.

GRANDMOTHER: Throw it in the fire?

EDDIE: I agree, Pop.

HARVEY: Fine.. *(He tosses it into the "fire".)* Then we'll burn it immediately.

GRANDMOTHER: Harvey! What have you done?

HARVEY: I burned Eddie's drawing, Mother.

GRANDMOTHER: I specifically asked to see it.

HARVEY: I'm sorry, Mother.

GRANDMOTHER: You disobeyed me, Harvey!

PAUL: Let me feel your pulse, Mother.

GRANDMOTHER: We don't disobey our mothers! We don't throw things in the fire!

PAUL: Shall I call Annie, Mother?

GRANDFATHER: *(To* JANE*)* She'll get over it. Always does.

PAUL: Do you need your pills, Mother?

GRANDMOTHER: I am furious at your brother, Paul! I am very, very cross.

HARVEY: *(Falling on his knees in front of her)* Oh Mother, please!

GRANDMOTHER: *(Getting up)* I can't talk to you, Harvey! I can't look at you! I have to lie down. *(She starts for the "stairs")*

PAUL: I'll get Annie. *(He hurries off.)*

HARVEY: Oh Mother, wait!

GRANDMOTHER: No, Harvey. I'm much too upset.

*(*PAUL *hurries back on with* ANNIE.*)*

ANNIE: Come, Missus

GRANDMOTHER: We don't wantonly destroy art in this house.

JANE: *(To* GRANDMOTHER*)* But the artist rejected his own work.

GRANDMOTHER: What?

JANE: Eddie feels that the drawing isn't up to his best work, and has asked that it be destroyed.

GRANDMOTHER: Did he? Did you, Eddie?

EDDIE: I did, Gog.

HARVEY: *(Low to* JANE*)* Thank you, Jane.

GRANDFATHER: *(Quietly)* She'll turn now. Watch her turn. *(To* GRANDMOTHER*)* Dear, the good Professor here tells me that Keats destroyed several of his poems because they weren't up to snuff.

JANE: We have to respect the artist's intentions.

GRANDMOTHER: Oh yes. Oh yes...

ANNIE: *(Placing a chair)* Here, Missus. You should sit.

GRANDMOTHER: Now I don't know what to think.

PAUL: *(To* HARVEY*)* Maybe it's better for you to tip.

HARVEY: Yes, we should tip.... I'll stop by tomorrow, Mother.

GRANDMOTHER: I don't know if I can see you, Harvey.

HARVEY: Oh Mother ...

GRANDMOTHER: It's all very well to talk about art, but you disobeyed me.

HARVEY: When may I see you then, Mother?

GRANDMOTHER: Possibly the day *after* tomorrow. Depending on my heart. I'll telephone when you can come.

HARVEY: *(Making up his mind)* No, I'll telephone *you*, Mother.

GRANDMOTHER: What?

HARVEY: I'll call when I can.

GRANDMOTHER: When?

HARVEY: Later in the week. I've got many other things to do.

JANE: *(Quietly)* Yippee.

GRANDFATHER: *(Low to* JANE*)* Well, well. That's something new.

GRANDMOTHER: I'm terribly sorry, but my heart is too heavy to give anyone a good night kiss.

(She goes off, with ANNIE.*)*

PAUL: Should we call Doctor Russell?

GRANDFATHER: She's fine, she's fine.

HARVEY: Let's go home, Jane.

JANE: If the car will start.

HARVEY: Good night, all.

(He and JANE *quickly say their goodnights and go.)*

EDDIE: *(To audience)* All the other goodbyes were pretty much the same, except for two, so we'll do those.

(The others go off, except for LAMBERT *who crosses quickly by* EDDIE.*)*

EDDIE: *(Stopping him)* Good night, Lambert.

LAMBERT: *(Shaking loose)* Screw you, Eddie.

EDDIE: Hey look, Lambert. I happen to think you're bad news. You stole my drawing, you embarrassed me in front of my family, and you almost killed my grandmother. But it's still Christmas till midnight tonight, so why don't we both make an effort to be better guys, and shake on it. O K? *(He holds out his hand.)*

LAMBERT: *(Holds out his hand as well. But when* EDDIE *tries to shake it, he gives* EDDIE *the finger.)* Perch and rotate, Eddie. *(He turns and goes off)*

EDDIE: *(To audience)* That guy obviously needs an appointment with a good medicine man.

*(*GRANDFATHER *comes on)*

GRANDFATHER: I neglected to give you your Christmas present, Eddie. *(Takes out his roll of bills, peels off one)* The usual five. Not enough these days for a growing boy, but your grandmother's way of life is cleaning me out.

EDDIE: Thanks, Gramp.

GRANDFATHER: There will be very little left when I die. I hope before that happens I'll have enough to send you away....

EDDIE: To military school?

GRANDFATHER: Good God no. But away from Buffalo. You could use a fresh start.

EDDIE: Thanks, Gramp.

GRANDFATHER: Oh, and this Indian blood thing...

EDDIE: It just got a hold of me, Gramp.

GRANDFATHER: You like to tease people with it, don't you, Eddie?

EDDIE: Sometimes. Maybe. A little

GRANDFATHER: What if I told you that it isn't true?

EDDIE: We don't have Indian blood?

GRANDFATHER: I made it up, after I married your grandmother.

EDDIE: Why?

GRANDFATHER: I'm not sure.... At first it was just to tease her. See? I'm a tease, too.

EDDIE: Why did you tease her?

GRANDFATHER: I wanted to bring her back to earth.

EDDIE: Did it work?

GRANDFATHER: I'll let a fellow teaser answer that..

EDDIE: No it did not.

GRANDFATHER: But I still held onto it over the years.

EDDIE: So there was no Fabiola? Ever?

GRANDFATHER: No sir. It was Prudence, all the way.

EDDIE: Gee.

GRANDFATHER: Are you disappointed?

EDDIE: I sure am.... What about Lambert?

GRANDFATHER: Oh he's the real thing. One quarter Indian blood.

EDDIE: The lucky stiff.

GRANDFATHER: Yes, but the poor lad is embarrassed of his roots. That's why he's so uncomfortable in his clothes.

EDDIE: Lambert's a pill, Gramp.

GRANDFATHER: No, now give the boy a chance. Bury the tomahawk, and bring him in with the other chaps.

EDDIE: We're too different, Gramp.

GRANDFATHER: We're all in the same tribe, Eddie. All of us here.

EDDIE: Oh no.

GRANDFATHER: Oh yes. Maybe not an Indian tribe, but a tribe nonetheless. We're a lost tribe, with peculiar old customs. Once you've left the reservation, you'll look back and realize that. And you'll be just as hungry as Lambert for outside folks to bring you in.

EDDIE: You think?

GRANDFATHER: I do. Eddie. So why don't you practice by being easier on Lambert?

EDDIE: *(Thinking)* I'll tell you this, Gramp. Wherever I go, I'm still going to say I've got Indian blood....

GRANDFATHER: Oh yes?

EDDIE: Even if it isn't true, it ought to be.

GRANDFATHER: That's one way of looking at it, Eddie.

(Sound of a car horn offstage)

GRANDFATHER: Hark! The Herald Angels sing ...Goodnight, Eddie.

*(*GRANDFATHER *kisses* EDDIE *and starts off.)*

EDDIE: Thanks for the advice, Gramp.

GRANDFATHER: Advice is cheap, Eddie. Following it is the tough part. *(He goes.)*

(Kitchen sounds from off)

EDDIE: *(To audience)* Then I heard the maids still slaving away in the kitchen, because my grandmother liked to have fresh home-made rolls every morning for breakfast. So the least I could do was go back and thank Annie, and Jean, and Nelly and Ralph for all their hard work. And wish them Merry Christmas, even if they hadn't really had one. *(He goes off.)*

*(*HARVEY *and* JANE *settle into their car.)*

HARVEY: *(Honking again)* Where is that boy?

JANE: Have faith. *(Pause)* Tell me about the drawing.

HARVEY: It was repulsive.

JANE: Oh dear.

*(*HARVEY *starts to laugh.)*

JANE: What? Why are you laughing?

HARVEY: It was also quite funny.

JANE: Tell me.

HARVEY: I'm not sure I can....

JANE: How about when we get home? Upstairs? With the shades drawn?

HARVEY: O K. I'll tell you then.

JANE: I liked how you handled it, by the way.

HARVEY: I liked how you saved the day.

JANE: *(After a moment)* You know something, Harvey? For a while lately, I've been thinking about leaving you.

HARVEY: Why didn't you?.

JANE: I was scared it would kill your mother.

HARVEY: It damn well might have.

JANE: But now I've decided to fight it out.

HARVEY: What changed your mind?

JANE: I realized that could kill her, too.

(He looks at her. She laughs. Then he laughs, too. EDDIE *comes out, now bundled up in overcoat and galoshes. He kneels again in back.)*

EDDIE: What's so funny?

JANE: Life. Life is funny.

HARVEY: Are we off, then?

JANE: We are off.

(We hear the sound of a tough start, then the motor catches. HARVEY *shifts carefully into gear. They lurch forward. For a moment, everyone sits lost in thought. The lighting might create a snowstorm effect here.* EDDIE *comes forward to the audience as the lights fade on* HARVEY *and* JANE.*)*

EDDIE: *(To audience)* And here you should see a 1941, battleship gray, eight cylinder Oldsmobile sedan, with white sidewall tires and hydromatic transmission, disappearing down Delaware Avenue between two beautiful rows of snow-laden American elms. But you can't show this on stage.

(Quiet music once again as the lights fade on EDDIE*)*

END OF PLAY

(For the curtain calls, a lively rendition of Shuffle Off to Buffalo *might be played. The family might be displayed as sitting for a formal photograph before taking the individual curtain bows.)*

www.ingramcontent.com/pod-product-compliance
Lightning Source LLC
Chambersburg PA
CBHW052207090426
42741CB00010B/2439

* 9 7 8 0 8 8 1 4 5 3 2 1 8 *